Better Homes and Gardens®
More Christmas Cookies

Contents

Pictured on the cover (clockwise from top left):
Thumbprint Tarts, Petal Cookies, Sandwich Cookies,
Two-Tone Quarter Cookies, Cranberry-Orange Spirals

Our seal assures you that every recipe in Better Homes and Gardens® *More Christmas Cookies* has been tested in the Better Homes and Gardens® Test Kitchen. This means that each recipe is practical and reliable, and meets our high standards of taste appeal.

BETTER HOMES AND GARDENS TEST KITCHEN ®

ISBN 0-696-20924-1

Sliced Cookies

Create a dazzling array of crisp, delicious cookies by combining four basic dough recipes with our ideas for shaping, filling and frosting. You'll find the recipes and variations through page 7.

Chocolate Cookie Dough

½	**cup margarine or butter**
½	**cup shortening**
1	**cup sugar**
⅓	**cup unsweetened cocoa powder**
¼	**teaspoon baking soda**
⅛	**teaspoon salt**
1	**egg**
2	**tablespoons milk**
1	**teaspoon vanilla**
2½	**cups all-purpose flour**

1. Beat the margarine or butter and shortening in a mixing bowl with an electric mixer on medium to high speed for 30 seconds. Add sugar, cocoa powder, baking soda, and salt and beat till combined. Beat in egg, milk, and vanilla till combined. Beat in as much flour as you can with the mixer. Stir in any remaining flour with a wooden spoon.
2. Chill about 45 minutes or till easy to handle. Follow shaping, chilling, and baking directions in the specific recipes.

For sliced cookies: Divide dough in half. On waxed paper or clear plastic wrap, shape each half into a 7-inch roll. Wrap and chill in refrigerator for several hours or overnight.

   Remove one roll from refrigerator. Unwrap and reshape slightly if necessary. Carefully cut dough into ¼-inch slices. Place slices 1 inch apart on an ungreased cookie sheet.

Bake in a 375° oven for 8 to 10 minutes or till edges are firm and dough has a dull appearance. Remove and cool completely on wire racks. Repeat with remaining dough. Makes about 50.

Sugar Cookie Dough

¾	**cup margarine or butter**
1	**cup sugar**
1	**teaspoon baking powder**
1	**egg**
1	**tablespoon milk**
1	**teaspoon vanilla**
2⅓	**cups all-purpose flour**

1. Beat margarine or butter in a mixing bowl with an electric mixer on medium to high speed for 30 seconds. Add sugar and baking powder and beat till combined. Beat in egg, milk, and vanilla till combined. Beat in as much flour as you can with the mixer. Stir in any remaining flour with a wooden spoon.
2. Chill about 45 minutes or till easy to handle. Follow shaping, chilling, and baking directions in the specific recipes.

For sliced cookies: Divide dough in half. On waxed paper or clear plastic wrap, shape each half into a 7-inch roll. Wrap and chill in refrigerator for several hours or overnight.

   Remove one roll from refrigerator. Unwrap and reshape slightly if necessary. Carefully cut dough into ¼-inch slices. Place slices 1 inch apart on an ungreased cookie sheet.

Bake in a 375° oven for 8 to 10 minutes or till edges are firm and bottoms are lightly browned. Remove and cool completely on wire racks. Repeat with remaining dough. Makes about 54.

For perfect sliced cookies

Manage the margarine

• Use only products that come in sticks and are labeled margarine. Do not use diet or soft products and those labeled spreads; they are not intended for baking and will not make satisfactory cookies.

• The type of margarine you use determines the firmness of your cookie dough and may change the way the dough should be handled. A 100 percent corn oil margarine makes a softer dough than others.

Chilling thoughts

• When you use corn oil margarine, chill cookie dough in the freezer for 1 to 2 hours or till it's firm enough to slice.

• You can speed the chilling process by freezing dough for about one-third of the refrigerating time. Do not freeze dough made with butter; it gets too firm.

• Keep half the dough chilled while you slice and bake the other half.

Keep in shape

• To keep dough in a perfect cylinder while it's chilling, slip a round drinking glass around each end of the roll toward the center.

• For round slices, rotate the roll as you cut.

• Reshape the slices with your fingers, if necessary.

Sliced Cookies

Whole Wheat Cookie Dough

½   **cup margarine or butter**
½   **cup shortening**
½   **cup granulated sugar**
½   **cup packed brown sugar**
½   **teaspoon baking soda**
¼   **teaspoon salt**
1   **egg**
1   **teaspoon vanilla**
1½ **cups all-purpose flour**
1   **cup whole wheat flour**

1. Beat the margarine or butter and shortening in a mixing bowl with an electric mixer on medium to high speed for 30 seconds. Add granulated sugar, brown sugar, baking soda, and salt, and beat till combined. Beat in egg and vanilla till combined. Beat in as much of the all-purpose and whole wheat flours as you can with the mixer. Stir in any remaining flour with a wooden spoon.
2. Chill about 45 minutes or till easy to handle. Follow shaping, chilling, and baking directions in the specific recipes.

For sliced cookies: Divide dough in half. On waxed paper or clear plastic wrap, shape each half into a 7-inch roll. Wrap and chill in refrigerator for several hours or overnight.

Remove one roll from refrigerator. Unwrap and reshape slightly if necessary. Carefully cut dough into ¼-inch slices. Place slices 1 inch apart on an ungreased cookie sheet.

Bake in a 375° oven for 8 to 10 minutes or till edges are firm and bottoms are lightly browned. Remove and cool completely on wire racks. Repeat with remaining dough. Makes about 54.

Peanut Butter Cookie Dough

¾   **cup creamy peanut butter**
⅓   **cup margarine or butter**
¾   **cup granulated sugar**
¾   **cup packed brown sugar**
¾   **teaspoon baking soda**
1   **egg**
3   **tablespoons milk**
1   **teaspoon vanilla**
2   **cups all-purpose flour**

1. Beat peanut butter and margarine or butter in a medium mixing bowl with an electric mixer on medium to high speed for 30 seconds. Add granulated sugar, brown sugar, and baking soda, and beat till combined. Beat in egg, milk, and vanilla till combined. Beat in as much of the flour as you can with the mixer. Stir in any remaining flour with a wooden spoon.
2. Chill about 45 minutes or till easy to handle. Follow shaping, chilling, and baking directions in the specific recipes.

For sliced cookies: Divide dough in half. On waxed paper or clear plastic wrap, shape dough into two 7-inch rolls. Wrap and chill in refrigerator for several hours or overnight.

Remove one roll from refrigerator. Unwrap and reshape slightly if necessary. Carefully cut dough into ¼-inch slices. Place slices 1 inch apart on an ungreased cookie sheet.

Bake in a 375° oven for 8 to 10 minutes or till edges are firm and bottoms are lightly browned. Remove and cool completely on wire racks. Repeat with remaining dough. Makes about 50.

Cookie Dough Flavor Variations

Spice (add with sugar): 1 teaspoon ground cardamom, ground cinnamon, apple pie or pumpkin pie spice. Or use a blend of ½ teaspoon ground cinnamon, ½ teaspoon ground ginger, ¼ teaspoon ground nutmeg, and ⅛ teaspoon ground cloves.

Citrus (add with egg): 1 teaspoon finely shredded lemon or orange peel.

Nuts (stir in after adding flour): ½ cup finely chopped walnuts, pecans, Brazil nuts, macadamia nuts, peanuts, cashews, or toasted almonds.

Coffee (add with eggs): 2 teaspoons instant coffee crystals dissolved in 1 teaspoon water.

Roll-Ins

1. Before chilling, brush rolls of dough lightly with water. Roll dough in:
   Finely chopped nuts, such as walnuts, pecans, cashews, Brazil nuts, peanuts, or roasted almonds.
   Wheat germ, grated or chopped shredded coconut, or slightly crushed granola. Chocolate-flavor sprinkles, colored sugar, or pearl sugar.
2. Slice and bake as directed in the basic recipe.

No time to bake the whole batch? You can store rolls of unbaked dough in the refrigerator for up to a week or in the freezer for up to six months.

Cranberry-Orange Spirals

1 **recipe desired cookie dough** (*from pages 3 or 4*)
1 **10-ounce package cranberry-orange sauce**
1 **teaspoon cornstarch**

1. Prepare desired dough; cover and chill till easy to handle.
2. For filling, combine cranberry-orange sauce and cornstarch in a small saucepan. Cook and stir over medium heat till thickened and bubbly; cook and stir 1 minute more. Cool; cover and chill.
3. Roll dough into a 16 × 12-inch rectangle on a floured surface. Spread filling to within ½ inch of edges. Roll up, jelly-roll style, starting from one of the long sides. Pinch to seal. Cut roll in half crosswise. Wrap in waxed paper or clear plastic wrap and chill for several hours or overnight.
4. Remove one roll from the refrigerator. Unwrap and reshape slightly if necessary. Carefully cut dough into ¼-inch slices. Place 2 inches apart on a greased cookie sheet.
5. Bake in a 375° oven for 10 to 12 minutes or till edges are firm and bottoms are lightly browned. Cool on cookie sheet for 1 minute. Remove and cool completely on wire racks. Repeat with remaining dough. Makes about 60.

Apricot Spirals

1 **recipe desired cookie dough** (*from pages 3 or 4*)
⅔ **cup finely snipped dried apricots**
⅔ **cup water**
⅓ **cup packed brown sugar**

1. Prepare desired dough; cover and chill till easy to handle.
2. Stir together apricots and water in a small saucepan. Bring to boiling. Reduce heat and simmer, covered, about 15 minutes or till water is nearly absorbed and the apricots are tender. Cool; mash apricots slightly. Stir in brown sugar. Cover and chill.
3. Roll dough on a floured surface into a 16 × 12-inch rectangle. Spread apricot mixture to within ½ inch of edges. Roll up, jelly-roll style, starting from one of the long sides. Pinch to seal. Cut roll in half crosswise. Wrap in waxed paper or clear plastic wrap and chill for several hours or overnight.
4. Remove one roll from refrigerator. Unwrap and reshape slightly if necessary. Carefully cut dough into ¼-inch slices. Place 2 inches apart on a greased cookie sheet.
5. Bake in a 375° oven for 10 to 12 minutes or till edges are firm and bottoms are lightly browned. Cool on cookie sheet for 1 minute. Remove and cool completely on wire racks. Repeat with remaining dough. Makes about 60.

Two-Tone Shapes

Prepare two cookie doughs (from pages 3 or 4) of contrasting colors; divide each dough in half. Form each half into a 7-inch roll. Wrap in waxed paper or clear plastic wrap and chill till easy to handle.

Two-Tone Halves: Using one roll each of two colors of chilled dough, cut each roll in half lengthwise. Press one half-roll of each color together with cut sides touching. Wrap and chill. Carefully cut dough into ¼-inch slices. Place slices 1 inch apart on an ungreased cookie sheet. Bake in a 375° oven for 8 to 10 minutes or till edges are firm and bottoms are lightly browned. Remove and cool completely on wire racks.

Two-Tone Quarters: Cut each half-roll in half again to form quarters. Reassemble, alternating colors and pressing so doughs adhere. Wrap and chill. Slice and bake as directed above.

Two-Tone Spirals

1. Prepare two cookie doughs (from pages 3 or 4) of contrasting colors; divide each dough in half. Cover; chill till easy to handle.
2. Roll one portion between two sheets of waxed paper into a 14 × 12-inch rectangle. Set aside. Repeat rolling with one portion of the contrasting dough. Peel top sheets of waxed paper from each rectangle. Carefully invert one rectangle over the other. Peel off waxed paper. Roll up, jelly-roll style, starting from one of the long sides. Pinch to seal.
3. Cut roll in half crosswise. Wrap in waxed paper or clear plastic wrap and chill for several hours or overnight. If you like, repeat with remaining dough, or, cover and chill remaining dough for other cookies.
4. Remove one roll from the refrigerator. Unwrap and reshape if necessary. Carefully cut dough into ¼-inch slices. Place slices 2 inches apart on an ungreased cookie sheet.
5. Bake in a 375° oven for 8 to 10 minutes or till edges are firm and bottoms are lightly browned. Cool on cookie sheet for 1 minute. Remove and cool completely on wire racks.

Sliced Cookies

Sandwich Cookies

**1   recipe desired cookie dough
(*from pages 3 or 4*)
Desired frosting (*recipes below*)**

1. Prepare desired cookie dough; shape into 7-inch rolls. Wrap and chill till easy to handle. Slice cookies slightly less than ¼ inch thick. Bake and cool as directed in basic recipe. Prepare frosting.
2. Spread the bottoms of half of the cookies with frosting. Top with remaining cookies, bottom sides down. Press together lightly.

Cutout Sandwiches: Prepare desired cookie dough; shape into 7-inch rolls. Wrap and chill till easy to handle. Slice cookies slightly less than ¼ inch thick. Using small hors d'oeuvre cutters, cut out designs in half the unbaked cookies. Place whole and cutout slices 2 inches apart on ungreased cookie sheets. Bake and cool as directed in basic recipe. Prepare desired frosting. Spread a plain cookie with desired frosting; top with a cutout cookie.

Liqueur Frosting: In a large mixer bowl beat ⅓ cup margarine or butter with electric mixer on medium speed for 30 seconds. Gradually add 2 cups sifted powdered sugar, beating well. Beat in ¼ cup crème de menthe, crème de cacao, amaretto, orange liqueur, or coffee liqueur. Gradually beat in 1½ cups sifted powdered sugar. If necessary, add additional liqueur to make spreadable.

Easy Fruit Frosting: Spread with one 8-ounce carton soft-style cream cheese with strawberries or pineapple. Store cookies in refrigerator.

Sour Cream or Yogurt Frosting: Combine ¼ cup dairy sour cream or plain yogurt; 2 tablespoons

margarine or butter, softened; and ½ teaspoon vanilla. Gradually beat in 2½ cups sifted powdered sugar. If necessary, add more powdered sugar to make spreadable. Store cookies in refrigerator.

Thumbprint Tarts

1. Prepare desired cookie dough; divide in half. Form each half into a 7-inch roll. Cover and chill in refrigerator several hours or overnight.
2. Cut cookie dough into 1-inch-thick pieces. Quarter each piece to form chunks. Place each chunk in an ungreased 1¾-inch muffin cup. Press slightly with thumb to make indentation.
3. Bake in 375° oven for 8 to 10 minutes. Cool in pans about 5 minutes. Remove with narrow spatula to rack.
4. Fill each cookie with a dollop of frosting; top with a piece of candied cherry. Makes about 50.

Or, use one of these filling ideas:
• Before baking, press miniature peanut butter cups or gumdrops into dough.
• Immediately after baking, press milk chocolate kisses; candy-coated regular, peanut, almond, or mint-filled milk chocolate pieces; chocolate-covered peanuts; or chocolate stars into dough.
• After baking, fill with frosting or nuts such as whole cashews, hazelnuts (filberts), macadamia nuts, pecan halves, or walnut halves. Drizzle with melted chocolate after cooling, if you like.

Stuffed Cookies

**1   recipe desired cookie dough
(*from pages 3 or 4*)
Desired frosting (*recipes follow*)**

1. Prepare desired cookie dough. Shape into 7-inch rolls, wrap in waxed paper or clear plastic wrap, and chill till easy to handle. Combine ingredients for desired filling.
2. Cut cookie dough carefully into slices slightly less than ¼ inch thick. Place half the slices 2 inches apart on ungreased cookie sheets. Place a rounded ½ teaspoon filling atop each slice (unless otherwise directed). Top each with a second slice, pressing edges with a fork to seal.
3. Bake in a 350° oven 8 to 10 minutes or till edges and bottoms are lightly browned. Remove to wire rack; cool. Makes about 30.

Fold-Overs: Prepare as above, placing filling on one half of one slice of dough. Fold slice in half over filling; press with fork to seal. Bake as above.

Currant-Nut Filling: Stir together ½ cup currants, ½ cup finely chopped walnuts or pecans, and 3 tablespoons orange marmalade. Makes 1 cup.

Apple Butter Filling: Stir together ½ cup apple butter and ½ teaspoon finely shredded orange peel. Makes ½ cup.

Butter-Brickle Filling: Combine ¼ cup butterscotch-flavored pieces and ¼ cup almond brickle pieces. Makes ½ cup.

Cream Cheese Filling: Stir together one 3-ounce package softened cream cheese, 1 egg yolk, 2 teaspoons sugar, and ½ teaspoon vanilla or ¼ teaspoon almond extract. Use a level ½ teaspoon for each cookie. Makes ½ cup.

Or, use about ½ cup jam, preserves, canned pie filling, or pastry filling.

Petal Cookies

1. Prepare desired dough, using recipes from pages 3 and 4. Form into four rolls about 1 inch in diameter. Wrap, chill, and slice. To shape, overlap slices slightly on cookie sheet to form three- or five-petaled shapes.
2. If you like, press a nut into center before baking or press a chocolate star into center after baking. Or, sprinkle with colored sugar or coarse sugar. Bake as directed in basic recipes.

Chocolate Trims

Chocolate-Dipped Cookies: Melt 2 ounces semisweet chocolate and 2 teaspoons shortening over low heat, stirring often. Dip half of each baked cookie into chocolate. Then dip chocolate-covered ends of cookies into finely chopped nuts or toasted coconut, if you like.

Chocolate Drizzle: Melt 2 ounces semisweet chocolate with 1 teaspoon shortening over low heat, stirring often till chocolate begins to melt. Stir till smooth. Drizzle over baked cookies.

Chocolate Ribbon Cookies

These striped cookies are as easy as patting doughs into a pan, then slicing the loaf.

- ½ **cup butter or margarine**
- ½ **cup shortening**
- 1 **cup sugar**
- ½ **teaspoon baking soda**
- ⅛ **teaspoon salt**
- 1 **egg**
- 2 **tablespoons milk**
- 1 **teaspoon vanilla**
- 3 **cups all-purpose flour**
- ⅓ **cup semisweet chocolate**

pieces, melted and cooled
- ½ **cup finely chopped nuts**
- ½ **cup miniature semisweet chocolate pieces**
- ¼ **teaspoon rum flavoring**

1. Beat butter or margarine and shortening in a mixing bowl with an electric mixer on medium to high speed for 30 seconds. Add sugar, baking soda, and salt; beat till combined. Beat in egg, milk, and vanilla till combined. Beat in as much of the flour as you can with the mixer. Stir in any remaining flour with a wooden spoon.
2. Divide dough in half. Into one portion, mix melted chocolate and nuts. Into the other portion, mix miniature chocolate pieces and rum flavoring. Divide each portion of dough in half.
3. To shape dough, line bottom and sides of a 9×5×3-inch loaf pan with waxed paper or clear plastic wrap. Press half the chocolate dough evenly in pan. Top with half the vanilla dough, then the remaining chocolate dough, then the remaining vanilla dough. Cover and chill for 4 to 24 hours or freeze for 3 hours.
4. Invert pan to remove dough. Peel off waxed paper or plastic wrap. Cut dough crosswise in thirds. Slice each third crosswise into ¼-inch-thick slices. Place 2 inches apart on an ungreased cookie sheet.
5. Bake in a 375° oven about 10 minutes or till edges are firm and bottoms are lightly browned. Remove cookies and cool on wire rack. Makes about 50.

Lemon-Poppy Seed Slices

Sandwich two of these delicate cookies together, or serve the wafers without the filling.

- ¾ **cup butter (no substitutes)**
- 1 **cup sugar**
- 1 **egg**
- 1 **tablespoon milk**
- 2 **teaspoons finely shredded lemon peel**
- ½ **teaspoon vanilla**
- ½ **teaspoon lemon extract (optional)**
- 2¼ **cups all-purpose flour**
- 2 **tablespoons poppy seed Powdered Sugar Icing (optional)**

1. Beat butter in a mixing bowl with an electric mixer on medium to high speed for 30 seconds. Add sugar and beat till combined. Beat in egg, milk, lemon peel, vanilla, and, if you like, lemon extract till combined. Beat in as much of the flour as you can with the mixer. Stir in any remaining flour with a wooden spoon. Stir in poppy seed.
2. Shape dough into two 8-inch rolls. Wrap in waxed paper or plastic wrap. Chill for 3 hours or till easy to handle. Cut dough into ¼-inch-thick slices. Place on ungreased cookie sheets.
3. Bake in a 375° oven for 11 to 12 minutes or till edges are golden. Cool on wire racks. If you like, spread Powdered Sugar Icing on flat sides of half the cookies; top with remaining cookies, flat sides toward icing. Makes 60 single or 30 sandwich cookies.

Powdered Sugar Icing: Stir together 1 cup sifted powdered sugar, ¼ teaspoon vanilla, and enough milk to make of spreading consistency. Stir in a few drops yellow food coloring, if you like.

Shaped Cookies

Buttery Spritz

Please all ages with this traditional holiday cookie.

- 1½ **cups butter**
- 1 **cup sugar**
- 1 **teaspoon baking powder**
- 1 **egg**
- 1 **teaspoon vanilla**
- 3½ **cups all-purpose flour**
  Decorative sugars, candies, fruits, or nuts (optional)

1. Beat butter in a large mixing bowl with an electric mixer on medium speed for 30 seconds. Add sugar and baking powder and beat well. Add egg and vanilla. Beat till well combined. Beat in as much flour as you can. Stir in any remaining flour with a wooden spoon. Do not chill dough.
2. Pack dough into a cookie press. Force dough through press onto ungreased cookie sheets. If you like, decorate with decorative sugars, candies, fruits, or nuts.
3. Bake in a 375° oven for 8 to 10 minutes or till edges of cookies are firm but not brown. Remove cookies and cool on wire racks. Makes about 84.

Almond Cream Spritz

Almond lovers will enjoy every bite.

- 1 **cup butter, softened**
- 1 **3-ounce package cream cheese, softened**
- ½ **cup sugar**
- ½ **teaspoon almond extract**
- ¼ **teaspoon vanilla**
- 2 **cups all-purpose flour**
  Finely chopped almonds

1. Beat butter and cream cheese in a large mixing bowl with an electric mixer on medium speed for 30 seconds. Add sugar, almond extract, and vanilla; beat till combined. Beat in flour. Cover

and chill dough for 30 minutes or till easily worked but not too stiff.
2. Pack dough into a cookie press. Force dough through press onto ungreased cookie sheets. Sprinkle with almonds.
3. Bake in a 375° oven for 8 to 10 minutes or till edges of cookies are firm but not brown. Remove cookies and cool on wire racks. Makes about 60.

Chocolate Spritz

Two different kinds of chocolate flavor these luscious cookies.

- 1½ **cups butter**
- 1 **cup sugar**
- ¼ **cup unsweetened cocoa powder**
- 1 **teaspoon baking powder**
- 1 **egg**
- 1 **teaspoon vanilla**
- 3¼ **cups all-purpose flour**
- 2 **ounces semisweet chocolate, cut up, or green candy-coating disks**
- 2 **teaspoons shortening**

1. Beat butter in a large mixing bowl with an electric mixer on medium speed for 30 seconds. Add sugar, cocoa powder, and baking powder and beat well. Add egg and vanilla. Beat till well combined. Beat in as much flour as you can. Stir in any remaining flour with a wooden spoon. Do not chill dough.
2. Pack dough into a cookie press. Force dough through press onto ungreased cookie sheets.
3. Bake in a 375° oven for 8 to 10 minutes or till edges of cookies are firm but not brown. Remove cookies and cool on wire racks.
4. Melt together chocolate or candy coating and shortening in a small heavy saucepan. Place cookies on waxed paper; drizzle with the melted mixture. Let stand till drizzle is set. Makes about 84.

Marble Spritz

Put both doughs in the cookie press at the same time. Every cookie will look a little different.

- ½ **recipe Buttery Spritz**
- ½ **recipe Chocolate Spritz**

1. Prepare Buttery Spritz and Chocolate Spritz doughs according to recipes. Do not chill dough.
2. Pack doughs side by side into a cookie press. Force dough through press onto ungreased cookie sheets.
3. Bake in a 375° oven for 8 to 10 minutes or till edges of cookies are firm but not brown. Remove cookies and cool on wire racks. Makes 84.

Peanut Butter and Jelly Spritz

If you plan to store these cookies, don't add the jelly until you're ready to serve them.

- 1 **cup sifted powdered sugar**
- ½ **cup creamy peanut butter**
- ½ **cup butter, softened**
- 1 **egg**
- 1½ **cups all-purpose flour**
- 3 **to 4 tablespoons strawberry or grape jelly**

1. Beat together powdered sugar, peanut butter, and butter in a large mixing bowl with an electric mixer on medium speed till smooth. Add egg; beat till well combined. Beat in flour. Do not chill dough.
2. Pack dough into a cookie press fitted with any blossom-shape plate. Force dough through press onto ungreased cookie sheets.
3. Bake in a 375° oven for 7 to 9 minutes or till edges of cookies are firm but not brown. Let cookies cool for 1 minute on cookie sheet. Remove cookies and cool on wire racks. Spoon a small amount of jelly into center of each cooled cookie. Makes about 50.

Clockwise from top: Buttery Spritz, Peanut Butter and Jelly Spritz, Marble Spritz, Almond Cream Spritz, and Chocolate Spritz.

Shaped Cookies

Brown Sugar Spritz

Serve some variety — try this version of traditional spritz which features brown sugar and lemon peel.

- 1   cup butter
- ½   cup packed brown sugar
- 1   teaspoon baking powder
- 1   egg
- ½   teaspoon finely shredded lemon peel
- ½   teaspoon vanilla
- 2⅔   cups all-purpose flour

1. Beat butter in a large mixing bowl with an electric mixer on medium speed for 30 seconds. Add brown sugar and baking powder and beat well. Add egg, lemon peel, and vanilla. Beat till well combined. Beat in as much flour as you can. Stir in any remaining flour with a wooden spoon. Do not chill dough.
2. Pack dough into a cookie press. Force dough through press onto ungreased cookie sheets.
3. Bake in a 375° oven for 8 to 10 minutes or till edges of cookies are firm but not brown. Remove cookies and cool on wire racks. Makes 70 to 80.

Orange Blossom Spritz

Look for orange-color decorating sugar to sprinkle over the oven-ready dough.

- ¾   cup butter
- ½   cup sugar
- 1   teaspoon baking powder
- 1   egg
- 2   teaspoons finely shredded orange peel
- ½   teaspoon vanilla
- 2¼   cups all-purpose flour
       Colored sugar, decorative candies, or nuts (optional)
       Orange Frosting (optional; recipe below)

1. Beat butter in a large mixing bowl with an electric mixer on medium speed for 30 seconds. Add sugar and baking powder and beat well. Add egg, orange peel, and vanilla. Beat till well combined. Beat in as much flour as you can. Stir in any remaining flour with a wooden spoon. Do not chill dough.
2. Pack dough into a cookie press. Force dough through press onto ungreased cookie sheets. If you like, decorate with colored sugar, decorative candies, or nuts. Or, drizzle with Orange Frosting if you like.
3. Bake in a 375° oven for 8 to 10 minutes or till edges of cookies are firm but not brown. Remove cookies and cool on wire racks. Makes 60.

Orange Frosting: Stir together 1 cup sifted powdered sugar, ¼ teaspoon vanilla, and 3 tablespoons orange juice. Add enough additional orange juice to make of drizzling consistency.

Christmas Ribbons

Give spritz a rainbow look with red and green food coloring.

- 1½   cups butter
- 1   cup sugar
- 1   teaspoon baking powder
- 1   egg
- 2   teaspoons vanilla
- ½   teaspoon orange or lemon extract
- 3½   cups all-purpose flour
       Red and green food coloring

1. Beat butter in a large mixing bowl with an electric mixer on medium speed for 30 seconds. Add sugar and baking powder and beat well. Add egg, vanilla, and orange or lemon extract. Beat till well combined. Beat in as much flour as you can. Stir in any remaining flour with a wooden spoon.
2. Divide dough into three portions. Tint one portion pink with a few drops of red food coloring and one portion light green with a few drops of green food coloring. Leave the remaining portion plain. Do not chill dough.
3. Pack dough into a cookie press, placing pink dough on one side, green on the other, and plain in the center. Using the ribbon plate, force dough through press onto ungreased cookie sheets. Cut into 2- and 3-inch lengths.
4. Bake in a 375° oven for 6 to 8 minutes or till edges of cookies are firm but not brown. Remove cookies and cool on wire racks. Makes 60.

Gingerbread Teddy Bears

For the beary best shape, be sure to form the balls into the sizes directed.

- **1** cup butter or margarine
- **⅔** cup packed brown sugar
- **⅔** cup dark corn syrup or molasses
- **4** cups all-purpose flour
- **1½** teaspoons ground cinnamon
- **1** teaspoon ground ginger
- **¾** teaspoon baking soda
- **½** teaspoon ground cloves
- **1** beaten egg
- **1½** teaspoons vanilla
  Miniature semisweet chocolate pieces
  Icing (optional; *recipe below*)

1. Combine butter or margarine, brown sugar, and corn syrup or molasses in a saucepan. Cook and stir over medium heat till butter is melted and sugar is dissolved. Pour into a large mixing bowl; cool 5 minutes. Meanwhile, combine flour, cinnamon, ginger, baking soda, and cloves. Add egg and vanilla to butter mixture and mix well. Add flour mixture, and beat till well mixed. Divide dough in half. Cover and chill at least 2 hours or overnight.
2. For each bear, shape dough into one 1-inch ball, one ¾-inch ball, six ½-inch balls, and five ¼-inch balls. On an ungreased cookie sheet, flatten the 1-inch ball to ½ inch for body. Attach the ¾-inch ball for head and flatten to ½ inch. Attach the ½-inch balls for arms, legs, and ears. Place one of the ¼-inch balls on head for nose. Arrange remaining ¼-inch balls atop ends of arms and legs for paws. Use chocolate pieces for eyes and buttons.
3. Bake in a 350° oven for 8 to 10 minutes or till done. Carefully remove and cool on wire rack. If you like, pipe on bow ties with Icing. Makes about 24.

Icing: Combine ½ cup sifted powdered sugar and enough milk or light cream (about 2 teaspoons) to make icing of piping consistency. Tint with one or two drops of desired food coloring.

Spicy Crinkles

Pictured on page 18
Sanding sugar has larger crystals than regular sugar. You can find it in specialty food shops and catalogs.

- **¾** cup shortening
- **1** cup packed brown sugar
- **1** teaspoon baking soda
- **1** teaspoon ground ginger
- **1** teaspoon ground cinnamon
- **½** teaspoon ground nutmeg
- **¼** teaspoon ground pepper
- **¼** teaspoon ground allspice
- **¼** teaspoon ground cloves
- **¼** cup molasses
- **1** egg
- **2¼** cups all-purpose flour
  Granulated sugar or sanding sugar

1. Beat the shortening in a large mixing bowl with an electric mixer on medium to high speed for 30 seconds. Add brown sugar, baking soda, ginger, cinnamon, nutmeg, pepper, allspice, and cloves and beat till combined. Beat in molasses and egg till combined. Beat in as much of the flour as you can with the mixer on medium speed, scraping sides of bowl occasionally. Stir in any remaining flour with a wooden spoon.
2. Shape dough into 1-inch balls. Roll balls in granulated sugar or sanding sugar. Place 2 inches apart on an ungreased cookie sheet.
3. Bake in a 375° oven for 8 to 10 minutes or till cookies are set and tops are crackled. Remove cookies from sheet and cool on wire rack. Makes about 60.

Chocolate Cordial Cups

These bite-size morsels are fancy but surprisingly easy to make.

- **½** cup butter or margarine, softened
- **1** 3-ounce package cream cheese, softened
- **⅓** cup sugar
- **¾** cup all-purpose flour
- **¼** cup unsweetened cocoa powder
- **2** ounces unsweetened chocolate
- **2** tablespoons butter or margarine
- **½** cup sugar
- **1** egg
- **1** teaspoon vanilla
- **1** tablespoon chocolate or coffee liqueur
- **2** tablespoons milk chocolate pieces

1. Beat the ½ cup butter or margarine and the cream cheese in a mixing bowl with an electric mixer on medium to high speed for 30 seconds. Beat in the ⅓ cup sugar. Add flour and cocoa; beat till well combined. Cover and chill about 1 to 2 hours or till easy to handle. Divide mixture into 24 balls. Press each ball onto bottom and sides of an ungreased 1¾-inch muffin cup.
2. Melt unsweetened chocolate and the 2 tablespoons butter or margarine in a small heavy saucepan over low heat. Remove from heat. Stir in the ½ cup sugar, egg, vanilla, and liqueur. Divide mixture evenly among muffin cups.
3. Bake in a 325° oven about 25 minutes or till set. Cool slightly; remove from pans. Cool completely. Melt milk chocolate pieces over low heat. Spoon about ¼ teaspoon of melted chocolate on center of each cup. Makes 24.

Bar Cookies

You can bake several kinds of bar cookies in the time it takes to make a single recipe of cutouts. Choose from (counterclockwise from upper left) Cashew-Topped Toffee Bars, Fig Chewies, Mincemeat Bars, Raspberry Cheesecake Bars, and Apricot-Almond Bars.

(Recipes begin on page 14)

13

Bar Cookies

Fig Chewies

Pictured on page 12
These easy bars are crowned with a delicate lemon glaze.

½   **cup packed brown sugar**
⅓   **cup butter or margarine**
½   **cup all-purpose flour**
¼   **teaspoon baking powder**
¼   **teaspoon ground mace**
1   **egg**
1   **teaspoon vanilla**
1   **cup chopped dried figs**
1   **teaspoon shredded lemon peel**
⅓   **cup chopped walnuts, toasted**
       Lemon Glaze (*recipe below*)

1. Heat and stir brown sugar and butter or margarine in a saucepan till butter or margarine is melted. Remove from heat; cool 5 minutes.
2. Stir together flour, baking powder, and mace. Set aside. Beat egg and vanilla into brown sugar mixture. Stir in flour mixture. Stir in figs, lemon peel, and walnuts. Spread batter in a greased 8 × 8 × 2-inch baking pan.
3. Bake in a 350° oven about 18 minutes or till set in center. Cool; frost with Lemon Glaze. Cut into bars. Makes 20.

Lemon Glaze: Stir together 1 cup sifted powdered sugar and 2 teaspoons lemon juice. Stir in enough water (about 1 teaspoon) to make a glaze.

Apricot-Almond Bars

Pictured on page 13
Reducing apricot nectar for the frosting intensifies the flavor.

⅓   **cup butter or margarine**
½   **cup packed brown sugar**
½   **teaspoon baking powder**
¼   **teaspoon baking soda**
½   **cup apricot nectar**
1   **egg**

1   **cup all-purpose flour**
¾   **cup toasted, chopped almonds**
½   **cup chopped dried apricots**
       Apricot and Cream Cheese Icing (*recipe below*)

1. Beat butter or margarine in a mixing bowl with an electric mixer on medium to high speed for 30 seconds. Add brown sugar, baking powder, and baking soda. Beat till combined. Beat in apricot nectar and egg till combined. Beat in flour. Stir in chopped almonds and chopped apricots.
2. Spread batter in a greased 11 × 7 × 1½-inch baking pan. Bake in a 350° oven about 20 minutes or till a wooden toothpick inserted near center comes out clean. Cool on a wire rack till room temperature. Frost with Apricot and Cream Cheese Icing. Cut into bars. Store in refrigerator. Makes 24.

Apricot and Cream Cheese Icing:
Gently boil 1 cup apricot nectar in a small saucepan about 8 minutes or till it is reduced to about 2 tablespoons; cool. Beat one 3-ounce package cream cheese, 2 cups sifted powdered sugar, and the reduced nectar in a small mixing bowl till smooth, adding more sifted powdered sugar, if necessary, to make of spreading consistency.

Pecan Pie Bars

Enjoy the flavor of pecan pie the easy way with timesaving bar cookies.

1¼   **cups all-purpose flour**
3   **tablespoons brown sugar**
½   **cup butter (no substitutes)**
2   **eggs**
½   **cup packed brown sugar**
¾   **cup chopped pecans**
½   **cup light corn syrup**
2   **tablespoons butter, melted**
1   **teaspoon vanilla**

1. Combine flour and the 3 tablespoons brown sugar. Cut in the ½ cup butter till mixture resembles coarse crumbs. Pat into an ungreased 11 × 7 × 1½-inch baking pan. Bake in a 375° oven for 20 minutes.
2. Meanwhile, beat eggs with fork. Stir in the ½ cup brown sugar, pecans, corn syrup, melted butter, and vanilla. Pour over baked crust, spreading evenly. Bake 20 to 25 minutes more or till set. Cool. Cut into bars. Chill to store. Makes 24.

Double Nut Bars

Surprise! These creamy bars need no baking.

½   **cup butter or margarine, melted**
¼   **cup granulated sugar**
2   **cups chocolate wafer crumbs (about 38 cookies)**
1   **8-ounce package cream cheese, softened**
¼   **cup butter or margarine**
⅓   **cup sifted powdered sugar**
½   **cup finely chopped pecans**
1   **teaspoon vanilla**
2   **tablespoons creamy peanut butter**
1   **cup sifted powdered sugar**
1 to 2 **tablespoons milk**
½   **teaspoon vanilla**
       Chocolate Drizzle (*recipe follows*)
       24 pecan halves

1. For first layer, combine ½ cup melted butter or margarine and granulated sugar. Add chocolate wafer crumbs; mix well. Press mixture into the bottom of an ungreased 8 × 8 × 2-inch baking pan; chill about 20 minutes or till firm.
2. For second layer, beat cream cheese and ¼ cup butter or margarine in a large mixing bowl

with an electric mixer on medium speed till mixture is fluffy. Add the ⅓ cup powdered sugar; beat till combined. Stir in chopped pecans and the 1 teaspoon vanilla. Spread over crumb layer. Chill about 30 minutes or till set.

3. For third layer, beat peanut butter and half of the 1 cup powdered sugar till combined. Add 1 tablespoon of the milk and the ½ teaspoon vanilla. Beat till smooth. Gradually add remaining powdered sugar, beating till smooth. Add additional milk, if necessary, to make of spreading consistency. Spread over cream cheese layer.

4. Drizzle with Chocolate Drizzle. Arrange pecan halves on drizzle. Cover and chill at least 2 hours before serving. Store in the refrigerator. Makes 24.

Chocolate Drizzle: Heat ⅓ cup milk chocolate pieces and ½ teaspoon shortening in a small saucepan over low heat till melted, stirring occasionally.

Raspberry Cheesecake Bars

Pictured on page 13
For a splendid ending to dinner, cut these bars into larger portions and serve them as dessert.

1¼ **cups all-purpose flour**
½   **cup packed brown sugar**
½   **cup finely chopped, sliced almonds**
½   **cup butter-flavor shortening or shortening**
2   **8-ounce packages cream cheese, softened**
⅔   **cup sugar**
2   **eggs**
¾   **teaspoon almond extract**
1   **cup seedless raspberry**

preserves or other preserves or jam
½   **cup flake coconut**
½   **cup sliced almonds**

1. Combine flour, brown sugar, and the ½ cup finely chopped almonds in a mixing bowl. Cut in shortening till mixture resembles fine crumbs. Set aside ½ cup crumb mixture for topping.

2. For crust, press remaining crumb mixture into bottom of a 13×9×2-inch baking pan. Bake in a 350° oven for 12 to 15 minutes or till edges are golden.

3. Meanwhile, beat cream cheese, sugar, eggs, and almond extract in another mixing bowl till smooth. Spread over hot crust. Return to oven and bake 15 minutes.

4. Stir preserves till smooth. Spread over cream cheese mixture. Combine reserved crumb mixture, coconut, and sliced almonds in a small bowl. Sprinkle over preserves.

5. Return to oven and bake 15 minutes more or till topping is golden brown. Cool in pan on a wire rack. Chill for 3 hours before cutting into bars. Store bars in refrigerator. Makes 32.

Mincemeat Bars

Pictured on pages 12–13
Enjoy the traditional holiday flavor of mincemeat in easy crumb-crust bars.

¾   **cup water**
1   **9-ounce package condensed mincemeat**
¾   **cup shortening**
½   **cup granulated sugar**
⅓   **cup molasses**
1¼ **cups all-purpose flour**
1½ **cups rolled oats**
    Powdered sugar (optional)

1. For filling, bring water to boiling in a saucepan. Add mincemeat. Reduce heat, cover, and simmer for 3 minutes, stirring often. Cool.

2. Beat shortening in a large bowl with an electric mixer on medium speed for 30 seconds. Gradually add granulated sugar, beating till fluffy. Beat in molasses. Add flour and beat till combined. Stir in oats with a wooden spoon.

3. Press half of the oatmeal mixture into the bottom of a greased 9×9×2-inch baking pan. Spread mincemeat filling over oatmeal mixture. Drop remaining oatmeal mixture by teaspoonfuls onto filling. Bake in a 350° oven for 30 to 35 minutes or till light brown. Cool in the pan on a wire rack. If you like, sprinkle with powdered sugar. Cut into diamonds or bars. Makes 24.

Bake the best bars

Think outside the square. Make triangles by cutting cookie bars into 2- or 2½-inch squares. Then cut each of the squares in half diagonally. For diamonds, cut straight lines 1 or 1½ inches apart down the length of the pan. Then cut diagonal lines 1 to 1½ inches apart across the pan, forming a diamond pattern.

Bar Cookies

Five-Way Fudge Brownies

Starting with the basic fudgy favorite, you can make five great variations.

½ cup butter or margarine
2 ounces unsweetened chocolate, cut up
1 cup sugar
2 eggs
1 teaspoon vanilla
⅔ cup all-purpose flour

1. Melt butter or margarine and chocolate in a heavy medium saucepan over low heat. Remove from heat. Stir in sugar, eggs, and vanilla. Beat lightly by hand just till combined. Stir in flour. Spread batter in a greased 9 × 9 × 2-inch baking pan.
2. Bake in a 350° oven for 20 minutes. Cool on rack. Makes 16 to 20.

Chocolate-Glazed Brownies: Prepare and bake Fudge Brownies as directed. For Chocolate Glaze, combine 3 tablespoons butter or margarine, 2 tablespoons unsweetened cocoa powder, and 2 tablespoons milk in a saucepan; cook and stir till mixture comes to boiling. Remove from heat. Stir in 1½ cups sifted powdered sugar and ½ teaspoon vanilla till smooth. Spread over cooled brownies. Cut into bars. Top each bar with a pecan half, if you like.

Peanut Butter Brownies: Prepare and bake Fudge Brownies as directed. For frosting, beat ¼ cup peanut butter till fluffy in a medium mixing bowl. Gradually add 1 cup sifted powdered sugar, beating well. Beat in ¼ cup milk and 1 teaspoon vanilla. Gradually beat in about ½ cup additional sifted powdered sugar to make of spreading consistency. Spread frosting atop brownies; sprinkle with ¼ cup finely chopped peanuts. Cut into bars.

Crème de Menthe Brownies: Prepare Fudge Brownies as directed, except omit vanilla. Stir ¼ teaspoon mint extract into batter. Bake as directed. For frosting, beat ¼ cup butter or margarine in a medium mixing bowl till fluffy. Gradually add 1 cup sifted powdered sugar. Beat in 2 tablespoons green crème de menthe. Gradually beat in about ½ cup sifted powdered sugar to make of spreading consistency. Spread atop brownies. Melt 1 ounce semisweet chocolate over low heat. Drizzle over mint frosting. Cut into bars.

Chocolate Chunk Brownies: Prepare Fudge Brownies as directed, except stir one 2.2-ounce bar milk chocolate, coarsely chopped, and one 2.2-ounce vanilla-flavor bar with almonds (Alpine bar), coarsely chopped, into the batter. Bake as directed. Cut into bars.

Caramel Nut Goodies: Prepare Fudge Brownies as directed, except stir ½ cup chopped pecans into batter. Sprinkle batter with ½ cup miniature semisweet chocolate pieces. Bake as directed. For caramel topping, combine one 6¼-ounce package vanilla caramels and 2 tablespoons milk. Cook and stir over medium-low heat till smooth. Drizzle caramel atop brownies. Cool completely. Cut into bars.

Cashew-Topped Toffee Bars

Pictured on page 12
The glossy chocolate topping is semisweet chocolate pieces melted right on the hot toffee bars.

½ cup butter or margarine
½ cup sugar
1 cup all-purpose flour
1 14-ounce can sweetened condensed milk
2 tablespoons butter or margarine
2 teaspoons vanilla
1 6-ounce package (1 cup) semisweet chocolate pieces
⅔ cup coarsely chopped cashews or peanuts

1. Beat the ½ cup butter or margarine and the sugar in a mixing bowl with an electric mixer on medium to high speed till mixture is thoroughly combined. Stir in flour. Press into the bottom of an ungreased 13 × 9 × 2-inch baking pan. Bake in a 350° oven about 15 minutes or till edges are lightly browned.
2. Heat sweetened condensed milk and the 2 tablespoons butter or margarine in a heavy medium saucepan over medium heat till bubbly, stirring constantly. Cook and stir for 5 minutes more. (Mixture will thicken and become smooth.) Stir in the 2 teaspoons vanilla. Spread mixture over baked layer. Bake for 12 to 15 minutes or till golden.
3. Sprinkle with chocolate pieces immediately after removing from the oven. Let stand for 2 to 3 minutes or till chocolate softens. Spread chocolate evenly over top. Sprinkle with cashews or peanuts. Cool. Before cutting, chill for 5 to 10 minutes or till chocolate layer is set. Cut into diamonds or bars. Makes 36.

Here are three versions of Five-Way Fudge Brownies. From top: Crème de Menthe Brownies, Chocolate-Glazed Fudge Brownies, and Peanut Butter Brownies.

Clockwise from top: Fresh and fragrant from the oven come Old-Fashioned Soft Sugar Cookies, Orange Cottage Cookies, and Spicy Crinkles.

18

Drop & Cutout Cookies

Old-Fashioned Soft Sugar Cookies

Because these cookies puff as they bake, select cookie cutters with simple, well-defined shapes.

1   cup margarine or butter
1½ cups sugar
2   teaspoons cream of tartar
1   teaspoon baking soda
½   teaspoon salt
3   eggs
1   teaspoon vanilla
3¼ cups all-purpose flour
      Colored sugar

1. Beat margarine or butter in a large mixing bowl with an electric mixer on medium to high speed for 30 seconds. Add sugar, cream of tartar, baking soda, and salt and beat till combined. Beat in eggs and vanilla till combined. Beat in as much of the flour as you can with mixer on medium speed, scraping sides of bowl occasionally. Stir in any remaining flour with a wooden spoon. Divide dough in half. Cover and chill dough for 3 hours.

2. Roll half of dough at a time on a lightly floured surface to ¼-inch thickness. Cut dough into desired shapes using 2½- to 3-inch cookie cutters. Place cutouts 1 inch apart on an ungreased cookie sheet. Sprinkle with colored sugar.

3. Bake in a 375° oven for 6 to 8 minutes or till edges are firm. Do not overbake. Cool on cookie sheet 1 minute. Remove cookies from cookie sheet and cool on a wire rack. Makes about 60.

Orange Cottage Cookies

You'd never guess that cottage cheese is a key ingredient in these moist cookies.

½   cup margarine or butter
⅔   cup sugar
½   teaspoon baking powder
¼   teaspoon baking soda
½   cup cream-style cottage cheese
1   egg
2   tablespoons milk
2   teaspoons finely shredded orange peel
½   teaspoon vanilla
1½ cups all-purpose flour
½   cup diced mixed candied fruits and peels
½   cup chopped candied red and green cherries
½   cup chopped pecans
      Pecan halves

1. Beat margarine or butter in a large mixing bowl with an electric mixer on medium to high speed for 30 seconds. Add sugar, baking powder, and baking soda and beat till combined. Beat in cottage cheese, egg, milk, orange peel, and vanilla till combined. Beat in as much of the flour as you can with the mixer on medium speed, scraping sides of bowl occasionally. Stir in any remaining flour with a wooden spoon. Stir in fruits and peels, cherries, and chopped pecans.

2. Drop dough from a rounded teaspoon 2 inches apart onto an ungreased cookie sheet. Press a pecan half into the top of each cookie dough mound.

3. Bake in a 375° oven for 9 to 11 minutes or till the tops spring back when lightly touched. Cool on cookie sheet 1 minute. Remove cookies from cookie sheet and cool on a wire rack. Makes about 48.

Swedish Butter Cookies

Dip part of each thin, crisp cookie in melted chocolate.

½   cup butter
¼   cup sugar
1½ teaspoons finely shredded lemon peel
¼   teaspoon vanilla
1   cup all-purpose flour
4   squares (4 ounces) semisweet chocolate
2   tablespoons shortening

1. Beat butter in a medium mixing bowl with an electric mixer on medium to high speed for 30 seconds. Add sugar, lemon peel, and vanilla and beat till combined. Beat in as much of the flour as you can with the mixer on medium speed, scraping sides of bowl occasionally. Stir in any remaining flour with a wooden spoon. Cover and chill about 1 hour or till dough is easy to handle.

2. Roll dough on a lightly floured surface to ⅛- to ¼-inch thickness. Cut dough into desired shapes using 2-inch cookie cutters. Place cutouts 1 inch apart on an ungreased cookie sheet.

3. Bake in a 375° oven for 5 to 7 minutes or till cookies just begin to brown on edges. Cool on cookie sheet 1 minute. Remove cookies from cookie sheet and cool on a wire rack.

4. Heat chocolate and shortening in a small heavy saucepan over low heat, stirring occasionally. Dip part of each cookie into chocolate mixture. Cool on waxed paper about 30 minutes or till chocolate sets. If necessary, chill cookies till chocolate sets. Makes about 40.

Drop & Cutout Cookies

Molasses-Date Drop Cookies

Crispy edges and chewy centers — that's what you'll find when you bite into one of these cookies.

½ **cup margarine or butter**
½ **cup shortening**
½ **cup packed brown sugar**
½ **cup granulated sugar**
¼ **teaspoon baking soda**
¼ **cup molasses**
1 **egg**
2 **teaspoons vanilla**
2 **cups all-purpose flour**
1 **cup pitted dates, finely chopped**
½ **cup chopped walnuts**

1. Beat margarine or butter and shortening in a medium mixing bowl with an electric mixer of medium to high speed for 30 seconds. Add the brown sugar, granulated sugar, and baking soda and beat till combined. Beat in molasses, egg, and vanilla till combined. Beat in as much of the flour as you can with the mixer on medium speed, scraping sides of bowl occasionally. Stir in any remaining flour with a wooden spoon. Stir in dates and nuts.
2. Drop dough from a rounded teaspoon 2 inches apart onto an ungreased cookie sheet. Bake in a 375° oven for 8 to 10 minutes or till edges are firm and bottoms are lightly browned. Cool on cookie sheet 1 minute. Remove cookies from cookie sheet and cool on a wire rack. Makes about 60.

Oatmeal, Raisin, and Walnut Cookies

Drizzled icing gives a festive look to these drop cookies, chock-full of raisins and nuts.

2 **cups rolled oats**
¾ **cup margarine or butter**
¾ **cup granulated sugar**
¾ **cup packed brown sugar**
1 **teaspoon baking soda**
½ **teaspoon ground cinnamon**
¼ **teaspoon ground nutmeg**
2 **eggs**
2 **teaspoons finely shredded orange peel (optional)**
1 **teaspoon vanilla**
1 **cup all-purpose flour**
1½ **cups raisins or one 8-ounce package chopped dates**
1 **cup coarsely chopped walnuts Powdered Sugar Icing (*recipe below*)**

1. For oat flour, place ½ cup rolled oats in a blender container. Cover and blend till reduced to a powder. Transfer to a small bowl. Repeat with remaining oats, ½ cup at a time. Set oat flour aside (you should have about 1½ cups).
2. Beat margarine or butter in a large mixing bowl with an electric mixer on medium to high speed for 30 seconds. Add granulated sugar, brown sugar, baking soda, cinnamon, and nutmeg; beat till combined. Beat in eggs, orange peel, and vanilla till combined. Beat in oat flour and as much all-purpose flour as you can with the mixer on medium speed, scraping sides of bowl occasionally. Stir in any remaining flour with a wooden spoon. Stir in raisins and dates.
3. Drop dough from a rounded tablespoon 2 inches apart onto an ungreased cookie sheet. Bake in a 375° oven for 8 to 10 minutes or till edges are lightly browned. Cool on cookie sheet 1 minute. Remove cookies from cookie sheet and cool on a wire rack. Drizzle with Powdered Sugar Icing. Makes about 42.

Powdered Sugar Icing: Mix 1 cup sifted powdered sugar, ¼ teaspoon vanilla, and enough milk (2 to 4 teaspoons) to make of drizzling consistency.

Grandmother's Jelly Cookies

Everyone will have sweet memories of Christmas when you serve these striking cookies.

1 **cup butter**
¾ **cup sugar**
1 **egg**
3 **cups all-purpose flour**
1 **slightly beaten egg white Finely chopped almonds and/or pearl sugar or granulated sugar**
¼ **to ½ cup currant jelly**

1. Beat butter in a large mixing bowl with an electric mixer on medium speed for 30 seconds. Add sugar; beat well. Add egg; beat till well combined. Beat in as much flour as you can. Stir in any remaining flour with a wooden spoon.
2. Divide dough in half. Roll one portion on a lightly floured surface to ⅛-inch thickness. Using a star-shape or scalloped round cookie cutter, cut into 2½-inch shapes. Roll out second portion to ⅛-inch thickness; cut with a 2-inch star-shape or scalloped cookie cutter. Using a ¾- or 1-inch cutter, cut a circle from center of smaller shapes. Reroll dough trimmings.
3. Brush tops of 2-inch shapes with egg white; sprinkle with almonds and/or pearl sugar or granulated sugar. Arrange all shapes on lightly greased cookie sheets; bake in 375° oven for 7 to 9 minutes or till bottoms are light brown.
4. Transfer to wire racks; cool. Place a small amount of jelly in centers of 2½-inch cookies; top with 2-inch cookies, sugar side up, and press together, showing jelly in center. Makes 36 to 42.

Gingerbread Cutouts

Youngsters love to decorate these cookies with raisins, red hots, and colored frostings.

½ **cup shortening**
½ **cup sugar**
1 **teaspoon baking powder**
1 **teaspoon ground ginger**
½ **teaspoon baking soda**
½ **teaspoon ground cinnamon**
½ **teaspoon ground cloves**
½ **cup molasses**
1 **egg**
1 **tablespoon vinegar**
2½ **cups all-purpose flour**

1. Beat shortening with an electric mixer on medium to high speed for 30 seconds. Add sugar, baking powder, ginger, baking soda, cinnamon, and cloves. Beat till combined.
2. Beat in molasses, egg, and vinegar till combined. Beat in as much of the flour as you can with the mixer. Stir in any remaining flour with a wooden spoon. Divide dough in half; cover and chill for 3 hours or till easy to handle.
3. Roll one portion of dough at a time to ⅛- to ¼-inch thickness on a lightly floured surface. Cut into desired shapes with 2½-inch cookie cutters. Place cutouts 1 inch apart on a greased cookie sheet.
4. Bake in a 375° oven for 5 to 6 minutes or till edges are lightly browned. Cool on the cookie sheet for 1 minute. Transfer to wire racks; cool. Makes 36 to 48 cookies.

Whole Wheat Gingerbread Men

Sugar and spice — that's what theses gingerbread men are made of!

½ **cup margarine or butter**
½ **cup shortening**
1 **cup packed brown sugar**
2 **teaspoons ground cinnamon**
1 **teaspoon ground ginger**
½ **teaspoon baking soda**
½ **teaspoon ground cloves**
⅓ **cup molasses**
1 **egg**
2 **tablespoons milk**
3 **cups all-purpose flour**
1 **cup whole wheat flour**
Powdered Sugar Icing (*recipe below*)

1. Beat the margarine or butter and shortening in a large mixing bowl with an electric mixer on medium to high speed for 30 seconds. Add the brown sugar, cinnamon, ginger, baking soda, and cloves and beat till combined. Beat in molasses, egg, and milk till combined.
2. Beat in as much of the all-purpose and whole wheat flours as you can with the mixer on medium speed, scraping sides of the bowl occasionally. Stir in any remaining flour with a wooden spoon. Divide dough into four portions. Cover and chill about 2 hours or till dough is easy to handle.
3. Roll dough, one portion at a time, on a lightly floured surface to ⅛-inch thickness. Cut dough using 3- to 4-inch people-shape cookie cutters. Place cutouts 1 inch apart on a greased cookie sheet.
4. Bake in a 375° oven for 5 to 6 minutes or till edges are firm. Cool on cookie sheet for 1 minute. Remove cookies from cookie sheet and cool on a wire rack; cool completely. Decorate with Powdered Sugar Icing if you like. Makes about 48.

Powdered Sugar Icing: In a small mixing bowl stir together 1 cup sifted powdered sugar, ¼ teaspoon vanilla, and 1 tablespoon milk. Stir in more milk, 1 teaspoon at a time, till icing is of piping consistency.

Sugar-Cookie Cutouts

These cookies make a great background for decorating.

⅓ **cup butter or margarine**
⅓ **cup shortening**
¾ **cup sugar**
1 **teaspoon baking powder**
1 **egg**
1 **tablespoon milk**
1 **teaspoon vanilla**
2 **cups all-purpose flour**
Powdered Sugar Icing (*recipe below*)
Decorative candies or colored sugar

1. Beat butter or margarine and shortening in a mixing bowl with an electric mixer on medium to high speed for 30 seconds. Add sugar, baking powder, and a dash of salt. Beat till combined. Add egg, milk, and vanilla; beat till well combined. Beat in as much flour as you can; stir in any remaining flour with a wooden spoon. Divide dough in half. Cover and chill for 3 hours.
2. Roll one portion of dough at a time on a lightly floured surface to ⅛-inch thickness. Cut into desired shapes with a 2½-inch cookie cutter. Place on an ungreased cookie sheet. Bake in a 375° oven for 7 to 8 minutes or till edges are firm and bottoms are very lightly browned. Cool cookies on a rack.
3. Frost cookies with Powdered Sugar Icing; sprinkle with decorative candies or colored sugar. Makes 36 to 48.

Powdered Sugar Icing: In a small mixing bowl stir together 2 cups powdered sugar, ¼ teaspoon vanilla, and 2 tablespoons milk. Stir in milk, 1 teaspoon at a time, till icing is of spreading consistency. Makes 1 cup.

*Kids will love selecting toppings for this easy
Brownie Pizza dessert made with a mix.*

Cookie Pizzas

What do you call a giant cookie that has a crust and toppings, is baked in a pizza pan, and cut into wedges for serving? A cookie pizza, of course! Serve these snazzy sweets at holiday gatherings, or include a few wedges on cookie gift plates.

Brownie Cookie Pizza

If marshmallows are one of your topping choices and you prefer them less toasty, add them the last 4 minutes of baking, instead of the last 8 minutes.

½   cup finely chopped nuts
1   15-ounce package fudge brownie mix
1½   cups assorted toppings (semisweet chocolate pieces; candy-coated milk chocolate pieces; tiny marshmallows; candy bars, cut up; small gumdrops, cut in half)

1. Grease a 12-inch pizza pan. Sprinkle with the finely chopped nuts; set aside. Prepare the brownie mix according to the package directions.
2. Carefully spread batter into prepared pan. Bake in a 350° oven for 15 minutes or till edges are set. Sprinkle partially baked brownie with desired topping. Return to oven. Bake 8 minutes more or till toothpick inserted near the center comes out clean. Cool on a wire rack. To serve, cut into wedges. Makes 16 servings.

Pecan-Praline Cookie Pizza

It's easier to cut this elegant dessert pizza before it's chilled.

¾   cup butter or margarine
¾   cup packed brown sugar
1   egg yolk
1   teaspoon vanilla
1½   cups all-purpose flour
¾   cup dairy sour cream
¼   cup packed brown sugar
½   teaspoon vanilla
16   pecan halves, toasted
½   cup chopped pecans, toasted

1. Beat the butter or margarine in a large mixing bowl with an electric mixer on medium to high speed for 30 seconds. Add the ¾ cup brown sugar and beat till combined. Beat in egg yolk and the 1 teaspoon vanilla till combined. Beat in as much of the flour as you can with the mixer. Stir in any remaining flour with a wooden spoon.
2. Spread dough in a lightly greased 12-inch pizza pan, slightly building up the edge. Bake in a 350° oven for 20 to 25 minutes or till golden.
3. Meanwhile, stir together sour cream, the ¼ cup brown sugar, and the ½ teaspoon vanilla in a small mixing bowl. Immediately spread over hot crust to within ½ inch of edge. Arrange pecan halves around edge of crust. Sprinkle with the chopped pecans. Cool thoroughly in pan on a wire rack; topping will set as it cools. Cut into wedges; serve when cooled. Refrigerate leftovers. Makes 12 to 16 servings.

Banana Split Cookie Pizza

This sweet pizza has many of the toppings of the soda fountain treat, but it's built on a cookie crust instead of ice cream.

¾   cup butter or margarine
¾   cup sugar
1   egg yolk
1   teaspoon vanilla
1½   cups all-purpose flour
1   8-ounce tub cream cheese with strawberries or pineapple
2   medium bananas, thinly sliced
⅓   cup chocolate-fudge, strawberry, or pineapple ice cream topping
⅓   cup drained maraschino cherries, halved
¼   cup chopped nut topping

1. Beat the butter or margarine in a large mixing bowl with an electric mixer on medium to high speed for 30 seconds. Add sugar and beat till combined. Beat in egg yolk and vanilla till combined. Beat in as much of the flour as you can with the mixer. Stir in any remaining flour with a wooden spoon.
2. Spread dough in a lightly greased 12-inch pizza pan. Bake in a 350° oven about 20 minutes or till golden. Cool in pan on a wire rack.
3. Just before serving, spread with cream cheese. Arrange banana slices over cream cheese. Spoon ice cream topping over bananas. Sprinkle with cherries and nut topping. Cut into wedges. Refrigerate leftovers. Makes 12 to 16 servings.

Cookie Pizzas

Chocolate-Cherry Cookie Pizza

Serve large wedges on dessert plates with scoops of vanilla ice cream, if you like, or cut smaller wedges for cookies. Be sure to use a pizza pan with sides to hold in the brownielike mixture.

¾ cup butter or margarine
¾ cup sugar
½ cup unsweetened cocoa powder
¼ teaspoon baking soda
1 egg yolk
1 teaspoon vanilla
1 cup all-purpose flour
1 10-ounce jar red maraschino cherries
1½ cups semisweet chocolate pieces
¾ cup sweetened condensed milk
⅓ cup chopped walnuts

1. Beat the butter or margarine in a large mixing bowl with an electric mixer on medium to high speed for 30 seconds. Add sugar, cocoa powder, and baking soda; beat till combined. Beat in egg yolk and vanilla till combined. Beat in as much of the flour as you can with the mixer. Stir in any remaining flour with a wooden spoon.
2. Spread dough in a lightly greased 12- or 13-inch pizza pan with a ½-inch edge. Drain cherries thoroughly, reserving juice. Cut cherries in half and arrange over dough.
3. Combine chocolate pieces and milk in a heavy medium saucepan. Stir over low heat just till chocolate is melted. Remove from heat. Stir in 3 tablespoons of the reserved cherry juice. Spoon and spread mixture over dough in pan, covering cherries. Sprinkle with nuts.
4. Bake in a 350° oven about 25 minutes or till edge of pizza is firm. Cool in pan on a wire rack. Cut into wedges. Makes 12 to 16 servings.

Rocky Road Cookie Pizza

Drizzled melted chocolate crowns this gooey cookie treat.

¾ cup butter or margarine
¾ cup packed brown sugar
1 egg yolk
1 teaspoon vanilla
1½ cups all-purpose flour
1¼ cups semisweet chocolate pieces
1½ cups tiny marshmallows
½ cup chopped peanuts
½ teaspoon shortening

1. Beat the butter or margarine in a large mixing bowl with an electric mixer on medium to high speed for 30 seconds. Add the brown sugar and beat till combined. Beat in the egg yolk and vanilla till combined. Beat in as much of the flour as you can with the mixer. Stir in any remaining flour with a wooden spoon.
2. Spread dough in a lightly greased 12-inch pizza pan. Bake in a 350° oven about 25 minutes or till golden.
3. Sprinkle hot crust with 1 cup of the chocolate pieces. Let stand 1 to 2 minutes to soften. Spread chocolate over crust. Sprinkle with marshmallows and nuts. Bake 3 minutes more or till marshmallows are puffed. Cool in pan on a wire rack.
4. Melt the remaining ¼ cup chocolate pieces and shortening in a small saucepan over low heat, stirring constantly. Drizzle over cooled pizza. Cut into wedges. Makes 12 to 16 servings.

Raspberry Cheesecake Cookie Pizza

Swirls of rich raspberry color make this a perfect dessert for the holidays.

¾ cup butter or margarine
¾ cup sugar
1 egg yolk
1 teaspoon vanilla
1½ cups all-purpose flour
1 8-ounce package cream cheese, softened
1 egg
1 tablespoon sugar
⅓ cup seedless raspberry preserves
¼ cup sliced almonds, toasted

1. Beat the butter or margarine in a large mixing bowl with an electric mixer on medium to high speed for 30 seconds. Add the ¾ cup sugar and beat till combined. Beat in egg yolk and vanilla till combined. Beat in as much of the flour as you can with the mixer. Stir in any remaining flour with a spoon.
2. Spread dough in a lightly greased 12- or 13-inch pizza pan. Bake in a 350° oven about 20 minutes or till golden.
3. Meanwhile, beat together cream cheese, 1 egg, and the 1 tablespoon sugar till smooth. Spread over hot crust to within ½ inch of the edge. Dollop preserves on top. With a knife, carefully swirl preserves to marble. Sprinkle with almonds. Bake 5 to 10 minutes more or till filling is set. Cool in pan on a wire rack. Cut into wedges. Store in refrigerator. Makes 12 to 16 servings.